ANIMAL IDIOMS

Eagle-Eyed: Are Eagles Sharp-Sighted?

BY LAURA PERDEW

CONTENT CONSULTANT
TRICIA MILLER, PHD
EXECUTIVE DIRECTOR
SENIOR RESEARCH WILDLIFE BIOLOGIST
CONSERVATION SCIENCE GLOBAL, INC.

Kids Core
An Imprint of Abdo Publishing
abdobooks.com

abdobooks.com

Printed in the United States of America, North Mankato, Minnesota.
102021
012022

Cover Photo: Shutterstock Images
Interior Photos: MNStudio/iStockphoto, 4–5; Ruslan Dashinksy/iStockphoto, 6; Shutterstock Images, 8 (left), 10–11, 24, 26, 28 (top); Eric Jennings/Shutterstock Images, 8 (right); Jerry Bouwmeester/Shutterstock Images, 12; Andreas Nesslinger/Shutterstock Images, 14; Ian Duffield/Shutterstock Images, 16–17; Michal Ninger/Shutterstock Images, 18; Stephen Earle/Shutterstock Images, 20; Bokeh Art Studios/Shutterstock Images, 22–23; Sergey Uryadnikov/Shutterstock Images, 28 (bottom); iStockphoto, 29 (top)

Editor: Christine Ha
Series Designer: Katharine Hale

Library of Congress Control Number: 2021941223

Publisher's Cataloging-in-Publication Data

Names: Perdew, Laura, author.
Title: Eagle-eyed: are eagles sharp-sighted? / by Laura Perdew
Other title: are eagles sharp-sighted?
Description: Minneapolis, Minnesota : Abdo Publishing, 2022 | Series: Animal idioms | Includes online resources and index.
Identifiers: ISBN 9781532196676 (lib. bdg.) | ISBN 9781644946466 (pbk.) | ISBN 9781098218485 (ebook)
Subjects: LCSH: Eagles--Juvenile literature. | Birds of prey--Juvenile literature. | Eyesight--Juvenile literature. | Animal instinct--Juvenile literature. | Idiomatic expressions--Juvenile literature.
Classification: DDC 598.942--dc23

CONTENTS

Puzzles can take a long time to complete.

Good Eye!

Mia and Ava started their puzzle right after lunch. They put together the edges first.

Mia wondered where the last edge piece was. She looked at all the pieces laid out on the table. The piece was nowhere in sight.

Individuals who are eagle-eyed usually are good at noticing small details.

Ava's eyes moved across the pieces. She was quiet. Then she shouted, "There! The piece is right there!"

She plucked the piece Mia was searching for from the middle of the table. "Wow, you sure are eagle-eyed!" Mia exclaimed.

What Are Idioms?

Eagle-eyed is an idiom. An idiom is a phrase that is often used in a certain language.

It usually means something other than the words that make up the idiom. *Eagle-eyed* describes a person who is very **observant**. But are eagles really sharp-sighted?

Eagles' Eyes

An eagle's eyeball is about the same size as a human eyeball. The bird's large eyes take up most of its skull. However, an eagle's eye differs from a human eye in important ways.

Eagle Eyelids

Eagles have two sets of eyelids. One pair lets them close their eyes. The other pair slides over their eyes every three to four seconds to keep them clean and moist. Since this pair of lids is clear, eagles can see even while the lids are over their eyes.

Eagle versus Human Eye Sockets

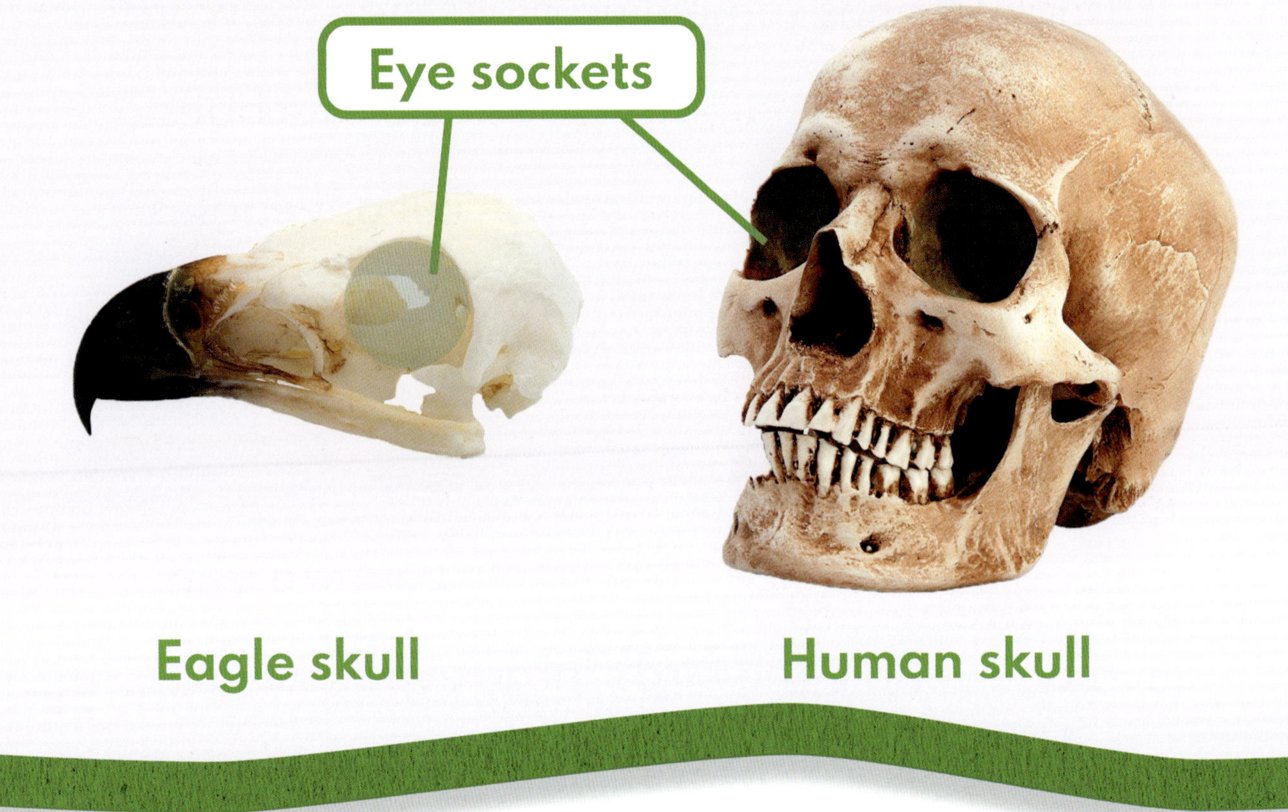

Eagles are much smaller than humans, yet an eagle's eyes are about the same size and weight as a human's. An eagle's eyes fill up most of its skull. The graphic above compares the eye sockets of an eagle and a human.

Eagles see a wider image than people do. One reason is their eye opening is round instead of oval like in humans. Another reason is the backs of their eyes are flatter than human eyes.

In addition, eagles have sharper vision than humans. That's because the **retina** in the back of the eye is different in eagles. An eye with more **cones** packed into the retina has sharper eyesight than one with fewer cones. Eagles have many more cones than humans. These features give eagles sharp long-distance sight, excellent **depth perception**, and a wide **field of vision**.

Further Evidence

Look at the website below. Does it give any new evidence to support Chapter One?

Eagles

abdocorelibrary.com/eagle-eyed

Photos that are taken at a high angle, like from a bird's perspective, are said to be taken at a bird's-eye view.

Distance Vision

Eagles have incredible long-distance vision. An eagle can see an ant on the sidewalk from the height of a ten-story building. It can see four to five times farther than humans.

Eagles are birds of prey. This means these birds hunt other animals for food.

At the doctor's office, a person with good vision can read an eye chart from 20 feet (6 m) away. That is known as 20/20 vision, which is considered normal. In comparison, eagles have 20/5 vision. That means what is clear to a human at 5 feet (1.5 m) away is just as clear to an eagle at 20 feet (6 m) away.

Top of the Class

All birds of prey have excellent eyesight. However, eagles are at the top of the class.

Eagle Vision Tests

In one study, scientists taught eagles to fly through a tunnel. At the end of the tunnel were two television screens. One screen had a striped pattern to attract the eagle. When each eagle landed on the striped screen, it was given a treat. The strength of the eagles' vision was tested by changing the width of the stripes and seeing from what distance the eagle turned to fly toward the correct screen.

Eagles hunt reptiles, fish, and small- to medium-sized animals. Some eagles may hunt bigger animals.

Their eyes are like binoculars. They can see tiny objects that are far away in great detail. Eagles can even spot a small fish below the surface of the water!

In addition, eagles can change their focus quickly. This is important for eagles as they fly and hunt for prey. They can keep their eyes focused on their food as they zoom toward it.

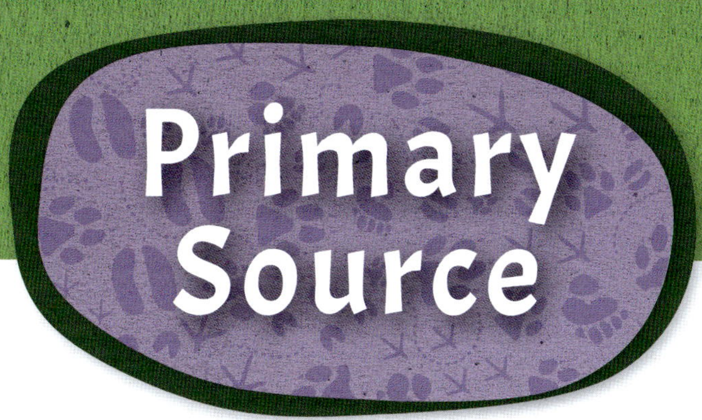

Raptors, including eagles, are birds that eat meat. The Peregrine Fund describes their eyesight:

> [Raptors] can spot medium-sized prey from at least 1 mile (1.6 km) away. That would be like spotting a rabbit across more than 17 football fields lined up in a row!

Source: "Keen Vision." *The Peregrine Fund*, n.d., peregrinefund.org. Accessed 2 July 2021.

What's thc Big Idea?

Read the primary source text carefully. What is its main idea? Explain how the main idea is supported by details, naming two or three of those supporting details.

Scientists estimate that eagle vision is about four to eight times better than human vision.

CHAPTER 3

Field of Vision

When people look forward, they have a 180-degree field of vision. They can see off to their left, straight ahead, and off to the right. In comparison, an eagle has a 340-degree field of vision. It can turn its head to see almost all the way around itself.

Eagle eyeballs are fixed in place. This means the birds cannot move their eyeballs within the sockets.

This is partly because an eagle's eyes are on the sides of its head.

Eagles also switch between binocular and monocular vision. Eagles use binocular vision to focus both eyes on one object at the same time. But eagles can use their eyes independently, too. This is called monocular vision. This allows eagles to look in two different places at the same time, giving them a wide field of view.

Eagle Eyebrows

Eagles have a big brow ridge over their eyes. It helps shade their eyes from the sun. However, it creates a blind spot. Because of the brow, eagles cannot see above them.

As an eagle dives to catch its prey, its eyes adjust so its sight remains focused and clear.

Depth Perception

Binocular vision gives eagles great depth perception. An eagle can see straight ahead and to the side at the same time. This is especially important when eagles make high speed dives for prey. Good depth perception allows birds to catch their prey without crashing.

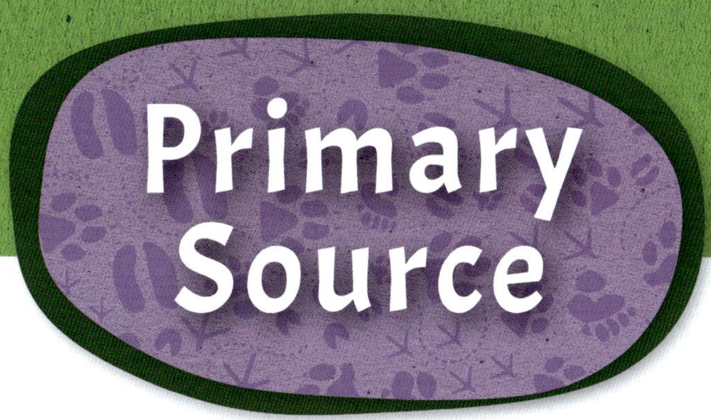

Francis Skalicky of the Missouri Department of Conservation observed:

> Eagles cannot move their eyeballs from side to side: Each eye is fixed in its socket. However, to compensate for this, a bald eagle has a greater range of head motion than a human.

Source: Francis Skalicky. "The Sharp Vision of Eagles." *Lake News Online*, 18 Jan. 2019, lakenewsonline.com. Accessed 2 July 2021.

Comparing Texts

Think about the quote. Does it support the information in this chapter? Or does it give a different perspective? Explain how in two or three sentences.

Humans can see about 2 to 3 million different colors. In comparison, scientists estimate that most birds can see about 100 million different colors.

CHAPTER 4

Color Vision

Birds, including eagles, can see the same colors humans do. But colors are much more **vivid** for them. They can also see many more colors. They can see more shades and tints of color than a human can. Shades and tints show how light or dark a color is.

In the summer, snowshoe hares turn a reddish-brown to help them blend into the forest ground.

Eagles' super color vision is due to the cones in their retinas. Cones are what allow an animal to see in color. Eagles have four cone types, while human eyes have only three. As a result, eagles can see a greater range of colors than humans.

Colors and Survival

Eagles can detect small differences between similar colors. They can also tell the difference between shapes. This ability helps them hunt. For example, the fur of snowshoe hares turns white in the winter. The hares blend in with the snow. But despite their white coats and the snowy landscape, an eagle can still spot them.

Night Vision

Eagle vision is better than human vision in many ways. However, eagles do not have better night vision. In fact, eagles and humans have similar night vision. This is why eagles hunt during the day.

Young bald eagles' eyes are brown. They lighten up to yellow as they grow older.

So, are eagles sharp-sighted? The answer is yes! Eagles have much sharper vision than humans. They can see farther. They have excellent depth perception, color vision, and a wide field of vision. Eagles have one of the best senses of sight in the world!

Explore Online

Visit the website below. What did you learn about how different animals see the world?

How Do Animals See the World?

abdocorelibrary.com/eagle-eyed

Eagle Facts

Eagles' eyeballs are about the same size as human eyeballs, but eagles have many more cones in the backs of their eyes.

An eagle can spot prey from a distance. It can also spot animals that are in water or blend into the land.

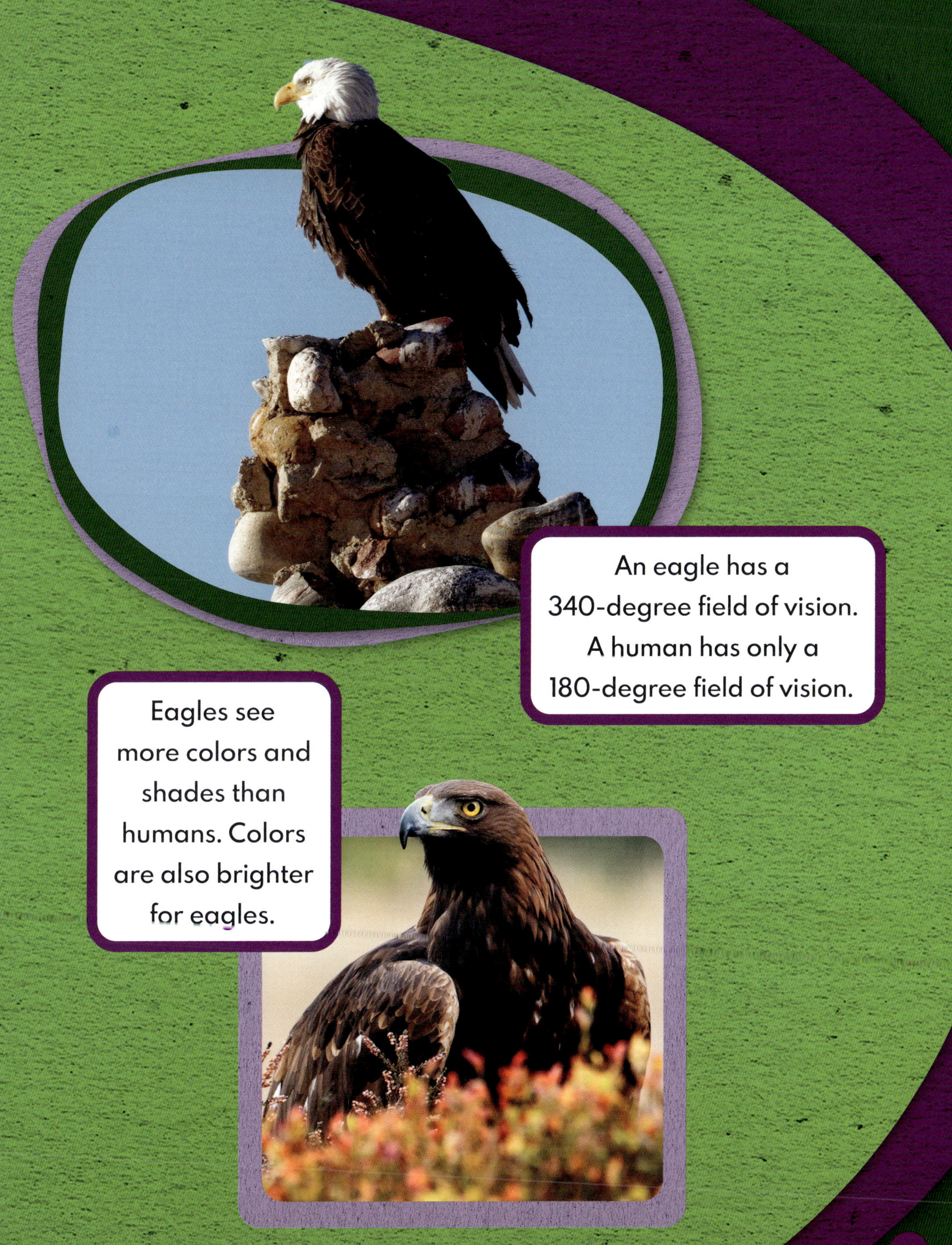

An eagle has a 340-degree field of vision. A human has only a 180-degree field of vision.

Eagles see more colors and shades than humans. Colors are also brighter for eagles.

Glossary

cones
cells in the retina of the eye that help an animal or human to see details and colors

depth perception
the ability to judge how far away something is

field of vision
the area a human or animal can see when looking in a fixed direction

observant
good at noticing things

retina
the layer at the back of an eyeball that senses light and color

vivid
bright and clear

Online Resources

To learn more about eagles, visit our free resource websites below.

Visit **abdocorelibrary.com** or scan this QR code for free Common Core resources for teachers and students, including vetted activities, multimedia, and booklinks, for deeper subject comprehension.

Visit **abdobooklinks.com** or scan this QR code for free additional online weblinks for further learning. These links are routinely monitored and updated to provide the most current information available.

Learn More

Markle, Sandra. *What If You Had Animal Eyes?* Scholastic Inc., 2017.

Murray, Julie. *Eagles.* Abdo, 2020.

Perdew, Laura. *Birdbrain: Are Birds Dumb?* Abdo, 2022.

Index

About the Author

Laura Perdew is a mom, writing consultant, and author of over 40 books for children. She writes both fiction and nonfiction with a focus on nature, the environment, and environmental issues. She lives and plays in Boulder, Colorado.